CAN YOU FEEL ME?

"Hurt Ain't No Joke"

Minister Easter M. Destin

Dedication

This book is dedicated to the memory of my Mother Rosetta Givens, Rev. Adam Mosley Sr. My Father, My sister Margaret Ann Brown, Brother Jerry W. Winfrey.

Published in the United States of America

Houston, Texas

Copyright © 2015 by Minister Easter Destin

Published by Minister Easter Destin

Book Design: LadyMpublishing

Introduction

Hello. I am Evangelist Eater M. Destin

This is a book of inspiring words to others. God inspired me to write these poems and it has been a blessing to me to share with others.

I never imagined that I would be writing to encourage others but, I love what I do. The greatest commandment that God wanted us to do is *"love ye one another as I have loved you."* He inputted in my heart is his love, there's no other way. We all have to be concerned, and compassionate towards one another. We can't make people love us if it's not there. So we have to continue to do our part. It breaks my heart to know that love don't feel the same.

There is much joy when you share love and happiness to others. You could only imagine; hurt ain't no joke! Life is only what you make of it. I've learned that people is going to be who they are, no matter what.

Love Always,

Evangelist Eater. M. Destin

November 21st, 2011

Hello my name is Minister Easter M. Destin. I am 54 years old. I should have started this a long time ago, but now is never too late. The topic of this book and poems is "Hurt Ain't No Joke."

The way I pronounce it is the way I mean it. I've been hurt several times, but not like these pains. Hurt comes in many ways, but the worst is right now. My childhood wasn't perfect. But there was foundation, structure and some love. There was a father and mother in growing up, sisters and brothers. I guess you would say, "Why am I hurting?" God told me in the spirit to write this book and poems to encourage others, and to understand my journey in hurt and pain. If you never felt what could cause a break down, let this happen while you're growing up. Not saying that I have others to blame but, behind every action is a reaction.

There were moments in growing up that there was good and bad days, that's all a part of being who you are. There are several hurts, no one wants to be hurt from anything or anyone. Some might would say we put ourselves in situations but some of this is out of our control. We have no control of people's thoughts and actions.

My thing is, I guess that everyone should have love in their heart for one another, but that's not so. God made me to be who I am, He gave me my heart, mind and soul.

I guess going thru this hurt, I should be mad, but I'm not. Just don't understand how people say that they love you but, yet they turn around and cause you hurt and pain. I'm not perfect but, I try so hard not to cause anyone to hurt or be in pain. When I was a young girl, I used to see others argue and fight and I be in the bathroom window looking and asking God why do they argue and fight? I guess at that time it seem funny to others but, not to me. I experienced love in high school. I mean, when someone showed me caring. This guy brought me a sweater, because I didn't have one. That was my first love of concern, you know it is a school girl crush; even though he was older than me. One day I looked up, he had left. I believe my father said something to him to make him leave. He was living with his grandmother, I hurt a while after that. Then I married my high school friend, but that didn't last. He left and went to the service, but didn't take care of me. Then I met my oldest son daddy, he was a truck driver. One thing about men is they show you the good side until they get you. Not knowing he liked to hit women; I loved him because I had my first child, a son. I had my son at the age of 21 years old. One day, because I didn't show him much attention, my son was like a week old, he slap me so hard that I almost drop my baby. I really start experiencing what it was to be abused by men. Then I had my second son from someone else, hurt ain't no joke. People claim that they love you; but deep down inside maybe they don't know what love is? With my second son, his daddy was cheating behind my back. I would go to work at night, he probably doing something different. He would abuse me mentally because it would be weeks before he would talk to me. He used to be a loving man too. So one day I just had enough and I went back home for a while. My oldest son daddy came by one day to visit, He said he wanted to take the boys to the store and he brought my youngest son back but wanted to take the oldest son to his mother to see his great grand-parents. Instead, he kept my son away from me for almost 1 year. I was sick, but I knew I still had to take care of my other son. But when you never experience what love supposed to be from home, what do you expect? I took so much abuse as a young woman. I refuse to take it anymore. I had wanted to hurt my oldest son daddy, but I just left and ask God to forgive him and my youngest son dad as well. What would I gain if I hurt them because of my heart? I felt then I was growing up. You can go thru so much in this sinful world that will cause you to make decisions about yourself. My parents tried to teach us about life's up and downs but, never warned us of the hurts and pains of growing up.

I had to learn that on my own. I've always worked. I started when I was at the age of 14 years old. My first job was at a Poppa Burger on Hirsch and Kelley Street. I start learning the value of money. You make it and spend it. But, thru it all, life sometimes deals you a bad hand. Hurt is a feeling you can't explain, sometime it comes at you slow and sometimes quick. You never know which way it enters.

In all my days I never experience the hurt I feel now. You can give all the love you got and expect it in return, but it don't happen like that. Jesus showed so much love that He died for us. He never said a word. I go thru it too and I hold my peace. And that's when it don't feel so good, hurt ain't no joke. I've never in my life want to cause no one no hurt or harm. I never tried to say anything that may cause a frown on their face. I'm not perfect, but I do have God's genuine love in my heart for people. I try never to do anything physically to cause any pain. I would rather know that I'm doing everything to please God and to bring love joy and happiness to someone's life. When I was a young girl I ask the Lord to never let me be mean to no one. I've been thru so much in my life that wasn't right in my life; men, drugs, being abused; but at the time it didn't matter. I was really hurting myself. Men, I thought they love me or say they did. But it was just to please them. But even in the midst of being hurt by them, I still wanted no harm to come to them. I just prayed for them. Love is action, but hurt is a disconnection from the person. Hurt causes you to run, to get away, it causes you to wonder. How is it people say that love you but, yet they cause hurt in your life. Not only men but people in general; there is always a lot of hurt. I understood when I was a child, they whip you because they say they love you to keep you from trouble. When I had my children that was a great love to give them a chance at life. I've tried to show them love with all my heart. I was not a perfect mom but I love my children. I gave them what money couldn't buy, love. It wasn't easy but, I never gave up. My last child I love her father because he gave me my daughter, not knowing he would abandon us. But, it's ok. I took care of my children until they grew up and got out on their own. I taught them to love, to share and be the bigger person and get a relationship with God. Because I'm not going to always be there. I always wanted to be a gospel singer. But it didn't happen. I went to beauty school got my license, then they expired. So, I just been working. I wanted to further my horizon more than just being a wife or a mother.

The opportunity came and went but, I never gave up. It hurts when you can't fulfill your dreams. *"The race is not given to the swift but to the one that endures until the end."* You know many times I try and get past other obstacles; but I know again, it's just a test of my faith. If I can learn how to stop helping those that hurt me, maybe I'll feel a little better. But, it's in my heart to be me. I don't have an evil heart or spirit, say if anyone is to be hurt, I would rather it be me. Like I say, I can go through the battle; it just don't feel good.

But Jesus didn't say it wasn't going to hurt. All that He went through, He continued to love and help and save. I thank God for loving me that He gave me chance after chance. Jesus don't hurt me but, He guides me through it. He give me strength when I don't think I have it. So many times I cry myself to sleep just thinking that I wish I could have accomplished my goals, but it's okay I'M STILL ALIVE! Through the beginning of my storms. HURT AIN'T NO JOKE, no matter who you are. We're living in a wicked world but, God gives us the power to change our situations. But, as long as you live, you're going to have hurt and harm. As I begin to grow, I really started to know Jesus for myself for who He really is. When I was young I heard about Him, but as I grow I learn about Him and know that I know Him. HURT AIN'T NO JOKE!

There's nothing comedy about it. It's an everyday struggle just to love, it's not hard for me to show love. Don't tell me you love me, show me. I sit and look at TV sometimes and smile, and sometimes it's sad. Lord, work on me to keep me from causing someone hurt and harm. Lord, deliver me from what people think about me. When I fall, because I am subject to make mistakes, don't judge me because you have issues too.

Marvin Sapp said in his song *"God see the best in me, when everyone else could only see the worst in me."* Endure, keep going, its ok if you fall. I have a heart that God planted in me, that's why it hurt when you don't love me back. As I love you in spite of. You see my fault but, you don't feel my love because you are blind to my inner man; which makes me so strong.

God hold me responsible for how I treat you all. So that's why I cry, because I can't do you no harm. I'm not perfect but, I am the one that God has chosen. It wasn't my plan. I just wanted to be me, like everyone else.

My reaction came behind your action, that's why I hurt. Hurt is nothing to laugh about or even cause some pain; but if they did it to

Jesus who am I? Don't' look at me wrong, don't point at me strong. Just remember He made me just like He did you.

Everyone have a different journey in life. Some are sweeter than others and some are bitter. But one thing I know, HURT AIN'T NO JOKE. A lot of my dreams don't come from the bottom. I only fall when I hurt. A hurt I can't handle but, only the strong survives. If you never been through nothing, how can you tell someone that God brought you out? Sometimes I sit and wonder, "How can you judge me, or talk about me and you had nothing to do with my existing? He made me to be someone that you don't understand. He knows my thoughts, my tears, my hurt and pain. He knows what make me laugh and what makes me sad. He love me no matter what. I beat myself up when I fall but, yet He loves me in spite of. Why is it that when you make mistakes or go through your trials, that's when I see you? I just begin to pray for you and ask you what I can do for you. There's no greater love than Jesus, so it doesn't even matter. Now when you mock me, at first I didn't understand how people can hurt you with their mouth and actions. And yet, they say they are God's children. I've experienced a deeper hurt that I never imagined. I've been through abuse, bad language, friends and family turn their back on me; I cried out for help but, no one paid me any attention. I hurt too, because I knew if they wouldn't hear me, the devil was right there to soothe my hurt.

Even in the midst of our hurt we tend to hurt others not realizing that we do. We have no control of others actions.

It was just a little while, while going through my hurt, a good friend of mine brought to my attention that my actions affected someone that was close to me; not being aware of how they felt.

From how I reacted out of being hurt, not realizing that her hurt was deep too; He brought to my remembrance when I was out there doing drugs or whatever that it hurt her real bad. All that I've been through, in her life, it affected her real bad and I'm so sorry. At the time all I could see was that I was done wrong. I gave my heart; yet to be stomped on, played with and taken for granted. I see why people do back ground checks on people. Hurt ain't no joke, you can try hard all you want people still going to be who they are, and it's nothing you can do about it.

You try to get past one stepping stone and here comes something else. There's no excuse for wrong doing but, it happens. I'm not making an excuse for my wrong doing but, it hurts. I never want my children to grow up hurting people, even though you get hurt. Just ask God to help you with the right decision. Always remember I raised you to love. It's so easy to run to wrong and we think it's a way out but, it's not. You just find yourself getting deeper in depression.

Transformation, that's a strong word and yet, it means so much. There is change for all of us. No matter what life brings us, we have to have on the whole armor of God. Sometimes God allow people to turn away from you. So you can continue to lean and call on him. I know what it means to cry out but, they don't hear. Have your way Lord in my life, it used to be dark in the daylight. I couldn't see my way clear I couldn't feel my way through period. I couldn't even begin to walk a straight and narrow path. Life brings on so many tribulations but, whatever choices we make there are consequences that have to come forth. Hurt brings on so many challenges, without my eyes I can't see the way, without my ears I couldn't hear the right thing. Without my hands and I couldn't hold on to what would keep me with a firm grip. Without my legs and feet my path would be limited. Without my head, my heart, my thoughts I would settle for anything; and without knowing what's right or wrong. I wouldn't know how to love in spite of, no matter what. I look at people in the world that have so many choices.

If you never been through nothing in life you don't know what it feels like to hurt for a reason. My mother have cancer and yet she's fighting for her life. I don't know what it feels but, I watch her in so much pain. I hear her mourn and cry. But yet, I don't know what's on her mind. Hurt ain't no joke. I can tell you of my pain or hurt but, I'm trying to understand. No one is no less than the other, sometime she lashes out at me and sometimes I don't understand why. But, everyday God gives me wisdom that she hurts and it's nothing she can do about it.

So, I have to stop being upset and accept it for what it is. It doesn't feel good to me, but God will get me through it.

When I started writing this book, I was in a dark tunnel trying to get through my hurt. I knew I couldn't do it by myself. No one could help me but God. It's like the date on a calendar counting down. And that's the way we have to take life one day at a time. You see people living under the bridge or on the street corner, they are going through pain for whatever their reason is for being there. I can't begin to know. I'm quite sure if they had some choices they would want a roof over their head, food on their table, a job and just knowing that they can be a part of society too.

I've never been there, hurt ain't no joke. My children are blessed, they never had to be without. It wasn't always easy or fair. But I tell you what, that are there children out there, that are their age, who would love to trade places with them.

They have probably been in the system of CPS all their life, not knowing where their parents are, or if there is anyone out there that love them; and will give them a chance to make something out of their life.

Hurt ain't no joke. No matter what we go through as parents; they are still affected from our pain. Have you ever wondered what it feels like to go in a store and you don't have enough money to feed your family, or have you ever wondered what it feels like to go to the hospital with no insurance? They check you in but, never get to see you for a while. Have you ever wondered what going to your pastor feels like, for advice, and he tells you he don't have time? Hurt ain't no joke. Have you ever been a child and you have to go to bed hungry, go to school and can't buy your lunch, so you stay outside pretending that you are okay, hurt ain't no joke.

So many reasons we fall into a hurt; not knowing what's next. You know her hurt ain't no joke. People don't realize the pain that causes on others and their mental stages and health. We all go through trauma in our life. But, we have to think before we open our mouth. We have plenty of time to weigh our actions.

Hurt sometimes feel like a sharp knife in your heart, or feel like someone has hit you with a lot; or even someone has passed away in your family that was dear to you. You can joke about many things in life but, it doesn't take affect like hurt. But yet sometimes we cry.

I have a son that had never been in trouble before, never gave me an ounce of a problem. But yet he was a child, a young man. Because of his decision in life, he caused some great hurt upon me; as well as, his family and himself. There are consequences behind every hurt that someone else have endured because of their actions. It was hurtful to him because he couldn't come to his grandmother or aunt's funeral. Hurt ain't no joke. No matter what happens, but I thank God that he sit him down so I wouldn't have to grieve over him. But it still hurts; then you have to watch them make wrong turns. But it's okay, because I had to learn. Then I had a brother's life taken away because of a stupid decision behind a female. Then the hurt caused his mother to have a slight heart attack and for our heart to hurt as well. Hurt ain't no joke whoever causes it. After the man shot him in his chest, he wrapped him up in a rug and took his body in a field and left him. But because he had my grandmothers phone number in his pocket, we were able to be contacted.

He left him as though he was a piece of meat, that's the way I felt. My father died from stroke and other illness. The grandchildren took it hard. They were close to their grandfather. I used to love to sing to him and travel with him to places he had to preach, I would drive. Our family stood on love; even aunts and uncles and cousins as well. I have a nephew that when my son left, told me "Auntie, I can't make it through without my cousin." He was talking about my son, and to be honest with you he went through a great hurt. Hurt ain't no joke, he just started to get it together. He went through hurt for seven and a half years. Now he has a job and he's getting ready to go to school. Tell me what action behind someone else's decision tell me don't cause hurt on another. Because you don't know how close your relationship is with someone. We can't take life for granted; we do affect one another, whether good or bad.

It's sad how you want the pay, but give no service. Jesus paid the ultimate price but, he served no matter what. I'm not perfect and I'm subject to fall and make mistakes. But I tell you what I have, God's love in my heart and spirit.

It doesn't matter what you say or think about me, I know who I am and whose I am. Hurt ain't no joke. I heard my baby brother say, "No matter if you are a minister or a man with a family. No one is exempt from wrong. But you go to that person and apologize get it straight there's no guarantee you will make it to the next day or even before the sun goes down. It's not about you being in high position or what just get it right." Hurt ain't no joke!

Ask God to restore your joy, give back your smile, and laughter is good for the soul.

When in the middle of the tunnel (your trauma) you begin to gain strength, not of the natural, but the spirit. Because God is the one to give you what you need. The race is not given to the swift but to the one that endures to the end. It doesn't matter how fast you want this to be over, we all have to go through the process no one is exempt. Ask God to direct your path. When you feel a little faint, say "Lord I need you. I feel a little weak, the pain won't leave. Lord hold my hand, while I run this race. Lord guide my feet so I won't continue to stumble." Don't let go, get a good grip. Don't let no one come in with their negative thoughts.

Because this is your breakthrough if you continue to stay focused. So many times we tend to take our eyes off the trial or situation and we get blindsided. Then we wonder what went wrong. Don't be like Peter, he got distracted and it caused him to fall. And believe me, it can happen even to the best of us. I've learned when you fall don't stay there, get up. Shake it off and start again. I found out that God is a second chance God.

God is a forgiving spirit, he loved in spite of all our downfall. He's not like man. Isn't it funny that when he gets ready to bring you out, and you feel the breakthrough that everyone is not going to be happy for you. Not you're so called friends, it's exciting when you know that God has delivered and set you free from the hands of the enemy. It's like in Matthew chapter 6, when he talked about the man that had leprosy, asked him, "Do you want to be clean?" Sometimes sin and being disobedient will cause you to be contaminated and you don't want to be around folks. But you have to be like the man and say," Yes I want to be clean, healed and delivered from my issues."

A lot of time people don't want to admit that they have issues. It don't always have to be drugs, it can be because you have nasty ways, hard heart, pointing the finger, causes someone to hurt. No one have room to talk about no one. But when God does it, he says tell no man. They won't believe you anyway. But you go show yourself, show them the evidence of how God brought you through.

Nobody but God can clean you up straighten you out and give you another chance. People love to hold your past over your head. But remember, you were once. I don't know if you ever experienced what I call church hurt. You wonder why people go from place to place. And as I grew up from childhood to adulthood you see so many things happen. I've always observed people, God gave me that. How people act towards one another, how they make them feel with their words. I hear people talk about their sisters and brothers in Christ. I was wondering at a young age is that the way it's supposed to be? But I kept on going to Sunday school, morning worship, BTU. Then the Word says train up a child in the way he should go, mean she too and they don't depart. Oh my God, things I observed I wouldn't want to treat people like that. But we so saved and sanctified, that we fail to realize they are baby Christians. We haven't always been where we are sometimes people just want to be a part of a Christian involvement where they two can make a difference. Hurt ain't no joke when people make you feel that they are the only one saved. But yet so far from being delivered from demons; when people come to the church they want to feel loved and accepted in the body of Christ. As leaders you play a big role in your flock's life, you are to lead as Christ led you and to be an example that they may follow. We are not always handed a life of royalty or get a good start, but make sure your past doesn't catch up with you in the midst of leading and teaching others. The old people used to say what goes on in the dark will come to the light.

I know about it, because I've experienced it several times. It's not a pretty picture, everyone seems to give you that look or talk about you. And wondering what's really going on with leadership. Sometime people or even family make you feel that God didn't choose you for a great work. How does your congregation bounce back from their leaders past or what they are doing that's not pleasing to God? How can they teach the word and not live it, as I stated before no one is perfect. But make sure your deeds are right with God; because it don't feel good to know your leader ain't right. Sometime I wonder do people go to these mega churches to hide from hurt and they don't have to be part of anything. Maybe they work in the church and wasn't recognized, because sometimes people over different departments feel they are the only one who can fill the position. They never give no one else a chance. Church hurt ain't no joke either. When you are truly delivered from whatever and you know without a shadow of a doubt, no matter what they say about you. You can stand and said. "Yes I was, yes I have that's my past and I'm living a righteous life now. You have to repent to God and in the spirit you will know. Where there's a 12-step with man but with God there's only one step. Hurt ain't no joke, no matter who it is or what. Just know God is in control. Lost, sinking deep in sin, but Jesus stooped down and real low and pick you up. It feels so good, you just want to tell somebody. Hurt ain't no joke. When no one sees the good in you. Okay, I'm going to go on another route now, relationships; whether marriage or dating.

Oh my God while laying here in my bed, the Spirit told me to get up and write some more. I was really relaxing. The Spirit wouldn't let me stay. I got up and went on my porch and started writing. God brought to me that no matter how you give your love you, are subject to be hurt. I'm learning through my experience of falling in love that it causes so many different reactions. That's why hurt ain't no joke. Women or men can give their all whatever it takes to make it work and someone still come up short. Love is real. It's nothing to take for granted. Whether in a relationship or just being kind to someone in giving a helping hand. Love is priceless, you can't buy love, and it comes from the heart. But if it's not in you, there will be no action for it. You have old love and you have young love. Old love come with time and age, you go through so much trying to build your marriage. You have to be patient, you have to have trust, and that comes from both sides. It's not a fifty-fifty it's a 100 percent. You both have to give your all. Men feel that they don't have to share their secrets but believe me you'll pay at the end. Hidden agendas will cause you to hurt at the end or even in your relationship. If you want to be with them the rest of your life, believe me, it's best to be for real.

Hurt ain't no joke, behind every action is a reaction, believe me I know. In a relationship or marriage, a person have a choice no one have the right to dictate your destiny. That's where the trust come in, if you want to deal with their past. Because if you don't, it will cause a major consequence in your life and in your relationship. Hurt ain't no joke. Whether it causes you not to be with a person to be serious.

You know I found it to be true, if it's not going to work, let it go. Even though the Bible say for better or worse, through sickness and death for richer or poorer. And I know God give us sense not to stay there, if a person is continuously hitting you, cutting up your clothes, breaking your windows in your car and you stay there, I can't see it. I know we all have issues but let me be real, something's are just too much.

Sometimes we stay in a relationship for all the wrong reasons. That's my baby daddy or mama, he or she gives me things; cars, home, money etc. But when it all comes to an end, when it all comes with time and age; things start fading away are getting old. The excitement gets stale, then what?

There's no more attraction, the money gets funny and the change is strange. Someone wants to step out and play around, then what? You might not know it to be true but something is happening, hurt ain't no joke. How can you keep it together?

If you are real about your marriage or relationship you both go into prayer and seek God for direction and answers. I know prayer will change things. When I was in a difficult relationship I didn't seek God for answers. I just wanted what I wanted; like so many others. But let me tell you, if I had mentioned at the middle or beginning of this book; The Holy Spirit told me not to but I wouldn't listen. I don't care how spiritual you think you are or saved you are. You go through things as well. You wasn't always where you are, it was a process you had to go through, even in your relationship or marriage.

But still hurt ain't no joke, no matter what you go through, even with life you go through as well. See God knew about my husband and I didn't and God knew it was going to hurt me dearly. Some love is blind. He said all the right things, done all the things I loved, especially with my ministry. I always wanted someone that loved God as hard as I did; especially when I was called and chosen by God to go tell the good news. Every woman or man want someone walking with them for God.

I have experienced too many times; when you're involving someone else in your circle, be true. It will pay off for right sometime. Once you lose that trust it's hard to get back, unless God help you with it. And I mean God really have to be in the midst of it. Hurt ain't no joke, just know what you have in your marriage or relationship that it's worth working at it. We all have a past and if you get past that; if you truly love one another, it can work out. Because I didn't think I would ever. But it was God that worked on me too.

My husband and I talked about the situation several times, because I want us to understand one another and let's pick up the pieces and shake it off and make it work. There's no perfect marriage, because there's no two people alike. We don't think the same. We do disagree, but not to the point of arguing and that's what I thank God for. Out of all my marriages and relationships I do have a man that truly love me. Never cursed at me, call me out of my name, or even put his hands on me; and that's a big plus in my marriage and my heart. So I'm hoping that couples know it's a process of falling in love. Me you don't know it all, we ladies know things to. God made us to be your helpmate not your maid or even your punching bag. But for us to love and respect you and for you to take care of us. But I do know all the kids are grown including his kids. and a few grandchildren. I'm going to enjoy now. I hope I can help some couple or young women or men before marriage or relationship. To the men and women, make sure he or she is the one.

Hurt ain't no joke. The Spirit came to me and said, when you get hurt it's a feeling deep down in your soul. It's something that no one wants to feel. When you have taken all you can take or handle from people (family friends etc.) It's no drug alcohol are doctors can help. Only God can give you that the inner peace. Hurt is like a knife that digs deep and cut close, it's a feeling that no one should experience.

Words sometimes cannot explain. Sometimes when I'm quiet and my mind get to wondering how people and things have gotten in my heart. But I cry, not wanting to get back at them. But to know hurt ain't no joke. Me, I cry my pain, try to make it go away. But only God with time will soothe the hurt. So anyone that goes through hurt it does not feel good. It's like a tattoo at that moment it won't leave or come off. But God!! Hurt ain't no joke. I'm continuing in writing I was trying to lay back down. But the Spirit, that inner man is telling me to write. We get in situations that we really don't want to be in, but things happen, people, and I know plenty, can they don't hurt or I'm not hurting at this moment. But I know they are lying. We all don't hurt the same but hurt ain't no joke, no matter what. I can't say enough that we don't have to run to the wrong direction, but it happens. Because we feel that we don't have to hurt no more. But after you come off the high, the problem of hurt its still there. I know. You can judge me all you want, but I have feelings too. And if you hurt me long enough or hard enough, I will feel. Believe me I won't hurt you physically or mentally for what, I could but why? Many of time it's just best to walk away and let God handle it. No one is perfect, not even you, whoever this might fit.

A lady told me, we were walking, that you are a woman of God, yes true, but like I told her I have feelings too. And she feel that I should be stronger. God made me in His image as a woman, but he also gave me feelings and

I hurt just like everyone else. I back track, fall, just like everyone else. No matter who I am, I'm only human. And to the saved Christian, you are too. You haven't always been where you are and whatever you are dealing with now you are just handling yours different. Why I say that, because I'm not in your house or even see you're hurt. But believe me, it ain't no joke.

I know so many people of God go through hurt and fall. So where do they run to, besides God? They are in their closets are in a dark place in their mind after being hurt or betrayed, and yet they have to run out too. God said in his word "judge not that thou be judged." That's why I don't point the finger cause I have no room to talk about no one. So many people I know think that they are all that and a bag of chips (smile). But one day your mountain will come crashing down, just let God keep waking you up no matter how old you are. Hurt ain't no joke. I listen very well at people conversation and I say that I'm so glad that I think before I open my mouth. You're not so young and surely not to old that you can say things that make you seem so right. I never, never want to say things that the ear have heard and it will cause a person to hurt or fall. Not realizing that it can, why, because you are not on the other end of the conversation. That they are talking to you, because they think you supposed to accept it. All the psychiatrist cannot heal a broken heart, they can tell you their solution, but if they never had a deep encounter of hurt deep down in their soul they don't know what it feels like or how to come out. Now if they have the connection of a relationship with the one and only God they can tell you. All the degrees on the wall cannot soothe you; unless you've been there. So as I stopped for a moment but not finish, I will be back. :)

Now you're just about at the end of your hurt, it's not as bad as it was at the beginning. God has given you a calmness that you never thought you would feel again.

Hurt ain't no joke, if you're not strong or have that relationship with God, you will lose your mind. When coming out you can begin to forgive the person that caused the hurt. You can get your joy back. God can restore you back; and it will be better than before. You would even start smiling, counting it all joy; not knowing where God is going to take you. I want to be like Job though you hurt me I'm still going to praise God. This joy that I have the world didn't give it to me and the world cannot take it away. So no matter what, don't give up; just keep pushing, God got his hands on you, stretching out for you, have his angels watching over you; keeping you covered with His precious blood. That no weapon formed against you shall prosper. It might form but it shall not prosper. Yea, though you walk through the valley and shadow of your situation, fear no evil because God is with you. Now I'm coming out as I see the light, I feel the warmness of God's love directing me out; showing me the way. It's been a long journey, I stumble and fell in this journey. I cried many days, months and nights, didn't know if I was strong enough but I didn't give up. Remember to look to the hills from which cometh your help all your help comes from God. When I look back over my life and I think things over, I can truly say that I've been blessed and I have a testimony. I rather have a testimony than a title anytime. Don't worry about where you've been, just know it is greater the second time around. I look at things different. I hear things clearly, my mind is open to receive good thoughts. I always want to treat people like I want to be treated with love, respect, compassion, and patience. Remember we all get hurt, no matter what. But there is always a way out and it's in Jesus he's the only one. We go in things in the natural but, before it's all over we're in the spiritual realm of God. No greater love that God would lay down his life for us. No one can love you like Jesus the Son of God. Weeping may endure for a night but joy cometh in a morning. Surely as it tarry, it is going to come to pass. As I get ready to exit from this, that hurt, just know it won't hurt much longer.

I want to tell you a story that my former pastor told about a baby and his Grandpa. I thought it would be nice to share it with you all. This baby was always crying but every time Papa would come into the room, he picked him up and he stopped crying and grand mama say," you need to stop picking him up and let him cry it's not going to hurt him." That bothered grandpa so much. He did it again grandpa said something to him and he stopped crying. So one day the baby was crying again and grandpa came in and he looked at the baby. So grandpa thought to himself that she said stop picking him up, but she never said I couldn't get in the play pen with him. Could you imagine that grown man in there. So that's the way Jesus is, He hears your cries, He see your tears. One thing I do know, no matter what you're going through; Jesus is just that concerned about you that He will get in the situation with you and bring you out. Nothing is too hard for God.

Darkness in life will cause you to hide yourself, your hurt, sin is darkness. Hurt ain't no joke. Just to be loved or even to love will cause you hurt. We never get prepared for pain, have you ever travel through a tunnel, I could imagine at the beginning it's dark, it might seem you don't know if you can make it through. And that's the way hurt and pain is. You can't even think that they would say they love you and yet they cause this hurt. You're saying," Lord I can't see my way through this, it don't feel good," even in the darkness God can shine some light on the situation. But you keep pressing in that tunnel. Obstacle are going to flare up. Because the enemy don't want your hurt to be at ease. Whatever it takes to keep you down that's his job. Hurt ain't no joke. You just continue to lean and depend on God for strength. Some hurt comes from not knowing a secret. In order to get over hurt, God has to get you through it, no one else. Man don't have the power.

It's so amazing how you can go from devastating to calmness in a situation. When everything has been broken whether material or your heart, it has to go through a process. It takes time to mend. It has to be broken down, refurbished, polished up, buffed and then sealed together. But with your heart it's a little tender. It's so amazing that all I've been feeling, through this I'm maturing at my age of 54 years old. Now I'm 56 years old. I was in a two year stand still after I lost my mother and my baby sister in the same month; hurt ain't no joke. But I know they will want me to get back to what I love feeding the needy, giving clothes, speaking his word praying for others. The joy of the Lord is my strength. My best teacher is God. In all your learning get an understanding. Life doesn't always deal you a good hand in growing up. The word says, the devil (enemy) go to and fro seeking whom he may devour, I know he's real. I used to be one of his employees; not trying to hurt no one. But doing what wasn't pleasing to God in the worst way, hurt ain't no joke.

In the word it says, we know not the day or the hour when he will come back. I tell you he has entered in my mind to write this book, but at the same time; I was growing up. The way I feel at this moment; I didn't think I would ever feel. I hope in reading this book and poetry, poems, that you feel what I am trying to say , don't take people feelings for granted. We all hurt too. I can't express it enough that behind every action is a reaction.

I hope that every woman and man that read this understand that a relationship is real in each other's lives. There is no two, it should be as one. You feel what I feel. You laugh, when I laugh. You cry, when I cry. You've been hurt as well as me. You really don't know a person until you live with them and then you still don't know. It's so amazing how, yet we were kids, young folks, babies and we get hurt and didn't understand. We knew we were going through something, but didn't know what it was. We cried, when it hurt. Wondering when it was going to stop? We asked why? Not understanding that when you grow up it gets worse. No matter what age you are, you will get hurt. Hurt ain't no joke. I say all the time I am like a rubber tree either way you bend, I'll pop back up. Only the strong survive, when something that you don't know about a person it is a secret or can you say is a hidden agenda? What makes it a secret, something that is hidden. A hurt not to be hidden, a secret is hoping that the one you told never tell. A hidden agenda may be something that you do not want to surface that may cause pain to someone that you know or to yourself. They called that a skeleton in the closet. When the young man and I was talking about secrets and hidden agendas, I got excited so many answers. It's a mind blower, a mind is a terrible thing to waste. Don't make it a part of your life to cause hurt to anyone. Life is too short to cause pain, our trials are to make us strong. We are overcomers by the word of God. So as God laid the path, let's build our life on the Word of God. Stop, look and listen, wait and pay attention!

And hear what the Spirit has to say. I say, hurt ain't no joke! I've grown up now and I will be more aware of my surroundings and everything I need on this journey and what God has equipped me with. I have the whole armor of God on now. My feet, and my mind are planted to follow and obey God. So my readers, it's been a joy in sharing my hurt, my heart and my joy with you; that no matter what life brings, you can make it through the hurt.

In my closing I have added some more of my writing, I hope you enjoy them. Don't ever give up on your dreams; no matter how old or how long it takes. It can be done. I love each and every one of you.

CAN YOU FEEL ME?

"Hurt Ain't No Joke"

Poems/Poetry

Minister Easter M. Destin

I Have A Dream

I have a dream that when God made me,
he made me special, he had a purpose
for me

I had a dream no matter what year I was
born that he knew my destination. When
I went through my changes he was
there, when I didn't know what I was
going to be he knew. I had a dream
whatever I grew up to be, he was going
to fulfilled it, because he knew what you
did.

So think, this is who I'm supposed to be
his beautiful daughter.

A Tear

A tear I shed not because of problems, not
because of pain. I shed tear for reason sometimes
I couldn't explain.

A tear I shed because I want things to be for the
good of others I shed a tea because it hurt so real,
because I love those that are near. I feel so deep,
I care unconditional that's why a tear I shed.

If you can feel me, if you could understand me, if
you could know where my heart lies, then you
would know what I'm saying

A tear I shed not for myself, but for you because
I want you to finally feel the peace that God has
given me, that's why

A tear I shed

Strength

Stand tall

Stand bold

But most of all be you.

It comes sometimes from out of nowhere. It's a feeling only you know no matter what happens it will take its place.

Sometimes we all have a meltdown, but for sure we know we can bounce back. Just reach up and reach out and grab what's yours.

Strength

A Chance

I take the high road of life but, yet I never know

the ending. If given the chance I will make it

worth my time. This way or That way, I won't

take it for granted. There's no limit to what I can

do, if I had a chance. Don't take my dreams

away, or my opportunity to be me. The journey

is wide. So I'll walk in it. If I had a chance, I

won't lose focus of what is real or not. Because I

don't have to be led to a dead end a chance will

come. Believe it or not. Take a chance

A Mother

She's the one that says OK. She's the one that prays for you when you need protection. She's the one that prepares your meal, and rubs your stomach when you feel ill.

She's the one that makes your clothes when the others you've out grown. She's the one who helps you study to make sure you stay on the right path. She's the one that tells you," Are you sure you want my life?" Then she returns in prayer again.

She's the one that shows you, life won't issue you a silver spoon so you have to get out and make a living for yourself. But remember at the end of your journey, she's still your mother.

Yes Me

I went through the valley, I even went through the storm. Life doesn't always pack fair, if it did you wouldn't be where you are.

I was once a baby

I was once a child

I was once a young girl

I was once a young lady

I am a mother, had the baby daddy drama.

Been through the drugs, been through the marriages.

Yes Me

So don't look at me strange, you've been through something too.

But I know someone who will love you in spite of.

Yes Me

Don't count me off, I'm finishing the race, I have the baton in my hand. It's Jesus. Yes Me

My Love

Come on in find your way around

Look here, look this way

Can you see? Can you feel where you're going?

It's big! It's great and it's smooth, my love.

I've never would imagine that my love would be taken

for granted.

I don't know no other way to be, because I'm just me.

Can you get a chance to wonder what it would be like

to give your love? It's priceless

That's me

My love been challenged

But guess what, that's me my love. My Love

Could You Imagine My Look

I didn't see it coming I didn't have a chance to

react Suddenly, I felt no need to escape.

But my soul was up in heaven.

"Could you imagine my look?"

So many around what a awful sound

Did I get a chance to exhale or did I fade away?

"Could you imagine my look?"

at that moment I looked over and saw their faces

in our own way we said we'll see each of later.

There was a calm atmosphere in the place,

nowhere to run or hide in but the bosom of God.

"Could you imagine my look?"

There was this white cloud a boarding us all

keeping us covered with his precious blood

"Could you imagine my look?"

I see your look, I feel your hurt, but we're all

okay now.

We're in a better place

"Could you imagine my look?"

We're smiling

There Are Times When I Sit Alone

There are times when my mind begins to rumble.

There are times no matter what you think, nor what you say.

There are times when it just don't seem right.

But one thing I can say I know there are times when I can have peace.

Can you hear the peace, can you feel the wind.

There are times you'll never know when it will arrive, the moment to be at ease.

You're done you're due, you've walk the walk, talk the talk. You moved unknowing, you've seen the impossible.

But there are times you never complain.

Now, enjoy it's your time.

My Mother / Our Mother

Can you imagine what she's worth?

Give her a kiss; give her a hug, could you
imagine what she loves?

Buy her a hat, buy her some food, but what
she has, you don't have enough.

She watched you grow, she watched you
sleep, she'll never go no where.

My mother/ our mother will give you
comfort in her arms, she will give you a kiss
in her love

But most of all she's my mother/our mother

She mean good all her days.

Do you see me?

Do you see me? I can see you.

You can't look through me, you can't open me up.

I see your smile, I see your tear.

You can turn around; you can go in and out.

Do you see me? I see you

I know your colors you have on, I know how you look,

sometimes your happy, sometime you're sad.

Do you see me? "I see you."

Let me tell you where I am.

I'm standing in front of you,

I'm that person you're not paying attention to.

Do you see me? "I'm that person, I see you."

A Smile

It's so easy, it's so big, it's like the sun that
shines in the day,

As the moon at night.

It's so easy to have one, just think of where you
came from and you will smile.

A smile will cause you to feel good, or even shed
a tear, because it's what makes me free.

Don't let no one steal our smile, because it cost
nothing.

Don't give the enemy yours cause he'll take…

to laugh at you!

A smile means so much to whom you meet
because you make them feel that they have one
too.

A smile

Window

Don't open

Just stand there, observe the view

What do you see while gazing abroad? It's so beautiful, it's so clear.

Window

I'm a special piece of art; I can

add beauty to your life. You can see so much, what are you focusing on? You can look beyond the dew that falls from a far.

Wipe it down, shine it up, place me and you can see the difference.

Just look out there so much around.

I'm here for you.

Don't Blame Me

Don't blame me for who I am.

You brought me into this world, you started me
on my way.

Don't blame me, because I didn't turn out the
way you thought I should. You taught me, you
guided me in an awesome direction. I am
wonderfully made I have grown to have thoughts
of my own.

Don't blame me because I chose to do the right
thing and have a life you never had.

I'm so glad I have choices

Don't blame me!

The Wind

Here I am sitting under a pine tree feeling the wind against my face. The air is so fresh, the sun is so bright, but the wind beneath my feet; like the clouds in the sky.

The wind you can't smell it, but you sure can enjoy it. It's a soothing to your thoughts, it's a wave that passes through your path.

The wind seems so unpredictable, but guess what, it never changes. Can you feel that inner peace that soother the soul?

The birds are chirping, the leaves are falling, the crickets are singing but the wind never stops.

Can you feel the wind? It takes you to another level where there's room for no wrong. Take a minute and feel the wind. You won't forget it.

Repent

Who Me?

Repent

Why Me?

Tell him you're sorry

Humble yourself

Repent

You can't get in

Repent

Don't you remember nothing but the pure in heart shall
see God?

Repent

He can make the difference

He won't bring it back up

Repent

And you'll see a change

21020914R00057

Made in the USA
San Bernardino, CA
02 May 2015